THE ESSENTIAL
CLASSICAL
COLLECTION
FOR SOLO PIANO

CHESTER MUSIC
part of The Music Sales Group
London / New York / Paris / Sydney / Copenhagen / Berlin / Madrid / Tokyo

Published by
Chester Music Limited,
14/15 Berners Street, London, W1T 3LJ, England.

Exclusive distributors:
Music Sales Corporation,
257 Park Avenue South,
New York, New York 10010 USA.

Music Sales Limited,
Distribution Centre, Newmarket Road, Bury St Edmunds,
Suffolk, IP33 3YB, England.

Music Sales Pty Limited,
120 Rothschild Avenue, Rosebery,
NSW 2018, Australia.

Order No. CH70587
ISBN 1-84609-226-4
This book © Copyright 2006 by Chester Music Limited.

Arranging and engraving supplied by Camden Music.

Printed in the United States of America.

www.musicsales.com

Your Guarantee of Quality:
As publishers, we strive to produce every book
to the highest commercial standards.

The music has been freshly engraved. Particular care has been
given to specifying acid-free, neutral-sized paper made from pulps
which have not been elemental chlorine bleached.

This pulp is from farmed sustainable forests
and was produced with special regard for the environment.

Throughout, the printing and binding have been planned to ensure a sturdy,
attractive publication which should give years of enjoyment.

If your copy fails to meet our high standards, please inform us
and we will gladly replace it.

CLASSICISM

Like all historical labels, classicism is a particularly awkward one. The classical era is said to fall roughly between 1750 and 1830 encompassing (along with the less significant works of their contemporaries) the works of Haydn, Mozart and Beethoven. The problem with the label 'classical' is that it implies a totally separate category from the romantic era whereas, in reality, there was a seamless transition from classicism to romanticism. Certain works of Haydn and Mozart might be said to display elements of romanticism, while Beethoven was seen by the romantic generation as the great prophet of the wild and unconventional new era.

It is important to remember that the term 'classicism' was coined in the 19th century (i.e. during the romantic era itself) in order to define the period before romanticism. In other words, it was a retrospective classification—Mozart, for example, never thought of himself as a 'classical' composer. In its original context, the term was used to identify a repertoire of classic works (especially those by Haydn, Mozart and Beethoven) which demonstrated mastery of every important genre including opera, the symphony, the concerto, the string quartet, the sonata, and sacred music. It was therefore, in a sense, the standard by which all subsequent work would be judged (and of course remains so to this day).

The word 'classical' is also used to imply a certain kinship with the classical art of antiquity. The new awareness of ancient models throughout the mid to late 18th century had a profound influence on art and architecture of the period. In the field of composition, this influence manifested itself primarily in composers' concerns about symmetry, balance and the perfection of large-scale musical structures.

The classical style might be said to represent a kind of synthesis of a number of different trends in European music in the mid 1700s. Significantly, J.S. Bach's sons, C.P.E. Bach and J.C. Bach led the way in rejecting what they considered to be the over-complexities of the high-baroque style as typified by their father's music. The new generation of composers were more interested in a simplified melodic style, their music tended to contain symmetrical eight-bar phrases and was clearly punctuated with simple cadences. During this transitional period, before the emergence of the mature Viennese Classical style, a number of stylistic trends arose including *Sturm und Drang* (literally 'storm and stress'), a style dependent on dramatic outbursts and a new emotional intensity (some of Haydn's earlier symphonies and sonatas show the influence of this style). On the other hand, the lighter *gallant* manner relied on a more elegant approach with simple symmetrical patterns and more than a whiff of courtly refinement.

Another key figure in the development of classicism was Gluck, who led the way in developing a new operatic style (comparable, although more limited in scope, with Wagner's a century later) in which the decorative excesses of the old-fashioned Italian opera were stripped away in favour of a new simplicity and emotional directness. His opera *Orfeo ed Euridice* (1762) displays a powerful range of noble expressivity, not least in its sublime 'Dance of the Blessed Spirits.'

Perhaps the most important development of the classical era was the emergence of a new kind of structure called Sonata Form in which two contrasting groups of thematic material are presented, developed and recapitulated in the most balanced and, at the same time, imaginative way possible. The skill required to compose a convincing piece in Sonata Form was the great challenge of the era, and the compositional devices of Sonata Form not only underpin all the instrumental genres of the period but permeate opera and even sacred music.

Haydn was the great consolidator of the classical period. A fantastically prolific composer (he wrote 104 symphonies and almost as many sonatas and string quartets) he achieved the perfect marriage of balanced form, stylistic control, imaginative genius and expression in nearly all his instrumental works. More than any other composer, he single-handedly established the string quartet as the major new genre of the classical style.

More than 20 years his junior, Mozart modelled his early work on the symphonies of J.C. Bach (the older composer befriended Mozart when he toured London at the age of eight!). But Haydn became his friend and mentor later in his career and declared to Mozart's father that he was the greatest composer of the age. Few would disagree with him. By the time of his death in 1791, he had shown complete mastery of every genre and had written the greatest operas of his age.

Beethoven was a pupil of Haydn's but the two never got on particularly well. Nevertheless, by the time Beethoven dedicated his first three piano sonatas to his illustrious teacher in 1796, he was already demonstrating superb mastery of Sonata Form whilst investing it with a new intensity and forcefulness. Coupled with his genius for writing slow movements that made contemporary audiences weep because of their new depth of emotion, Beethoven (even in his early works) was paving the way for the new romantic style.

CLASSICAL COMPOSERS

Ludwig van Beethoven (1770–1827) was born in Bonn but spent most of his working career in Vienna. His youthful genius was noticed by Mozart who died before he could give the boy lessons. Later, in the 1790s, Beethoven received tuition from the elderly Haydn with whom he had frequent disagreements.

Beethoven's talent burst on to the Viennese musical scene with the publication of his early piano sonatas and chamber works, all of which revealed a superb freshness in their handling of classical form coupled with a new intensity and force of personality. Even his early works were recognised as the products of an admittedly fiery genius and Beethoven, throughout his career, had the support of a number of enlightened aristocrats who supported him financially.

Beethoven's increasing deafness from 1802 onwards forced him to become reclusive. Increasingly eccentric and chaotic in his domestic affairs, he nevertheless produced a body of work, including a cycle of nine symphonies, seven concertos, 16 string quartets, an opera *Fidelio* and 32 piano sonatas that have a canonical status in western classical music.

Georg Benda (1722–1795) was a Bohemian composer and violinist. He specialised in opera and his work had many admirers in the 18th century, including Mozart whose short opera *Zaide* was much influenced by Benda's music.

In his most famous operas, *Ariadne auf Naxos* and *Medea,* Benda pioneered an experimental new device in which spoken dialogue takes place over orchestral accompaniment. His works were widely imitated.

Muzio Clementi (1752–1832) was an Italian-born English composer, pianist, teacher, publisher and piano manufacturer. He was adopted by an English gentleman in the 1760s and lived in Dorset where he studied music in isolation. Moving to London in 1774, he worked briefly as a conductor at the King's Theatre before touring Europe as a keyboard virtuoso and taking part in a famous contest with Mozart.

Clementi's numerous sonatas, along with his notorious piano studies, are an important part of the keyboard repertoire and were greatly admired by Beethoven (who preferred them to Mozart's).

Jan Ladislav Dussek (1760–1812) was a Bohemian composer of considerable gifts, admired by Haydn and Beethoven.

Having taken keyboard lessons with C.P.E. Bach in 1782, Dussek travelled through Europe, eventually settling in London where he set up a publishing company. When this went bankrupt in 1799, he returned to Germany and finally France where he ended his career in the service of the French statesman, Talleyrand.

His keyboard sonatas and chamber music are rooted in the classical style but his daring harmony foreshadows the romanticism of Weber and even Chopin.

Christopher Willibald Gluck (1714–1787) was one of the great composers of the classical era. As a child, he mastered several instruments and later in his career he became a virtuoso on the glass harmonica. However it was in his numerous operas that Gluck established a major reputation.

His most famous work, *Orfeo ed Euridice,* revolutionised 18th-century opera with its new simplicity of vocal writing, beauty of melodic writing and dramatic intensity. All these virtues were strikingly new during a period when opera had become somewhat decadent. Gluck's achievement influenced his operatic successors: notably Mozart, and later on Berlioz and Wagner.

Joseph Haydn (1732–1809) was one of the greatest composers of the classical era. The son of a wheel-wright, the young Haydn became a chorister in the Choir of St Stephen's Cathedral, Vienna, in 1740. Dismissed from the choir—because of his fondness for practical jokes—Haydn was forced to eke out his existence in Vienna as an itinerant musician.

With extraordinary diligence and enterprise, Haydn devoted himself to the study of theoretical works and the scores of C.P.E. Bach, rapidly building his reputation as a composer of talent. In 1761 he became court composer to the Duke of Esterhazy, a post he held for 30 years. During this time he composed the majority of his 104 symphonies, numerous operas, piano sonatas and chamber works, including his pioneering series of string quartets.

When Haydn embarked on his famous London tours in the 1790s he was already the most celebrated composer in Europe. Since his lifetime his works have remained models of classical excellence with their astonishing imaginative variety, wit, formal control and emotional depth.

Johann Nepomuk Hummel (1778–1837) was one of the most important composers of the early 19th century. An infant prodigy, his gifts were recognised by Mozart who gave him keyboard and composition lessons. As a travelling virtuoso, Hummel became famous throughout Europe. He settled in Vienna in 1793 where he received further tuition from Haydn and became a serious rival to Beethoven, with whom he had a stormy friendship.

Hummel's music is exceptionally well written in a clear classical idiom but his adventurous harmony foreshadows later romantic composers. His keyboard writing strongly influenced the young Chopin.

Friedrich Kuhlau (1786–1832) was a German-born Danish composer. To avoid subscription in Napoleon's army, he fled to Copenhagen where he became a successful pianist and teacher. His piano concertos and operas won him local fame. In 1825 he travelled to Austria and met Beethoven. Kuhlau's most famous theatrical work *The Elf Hill* (1828) contains a melody that now serves as the Danish national anthem.

Wolfgang Amadeus Mozart (1756–1791) was the son of Leopold Mozart, a court composer and theoretician. The young Wolfgang benefited from his father's instruction to the extent that he was composing keyboard pieces by the age of six. Thereafter, Leopold toured all the courts of Europe with his son, whose prodigious gifts were widely acclaimed in fashionable society.

The young Mozart learned his craft during his long stays in Rome, Paris and London. By the time he returned home to Salzburg in 1778 he was a brilliant young composer. After quarrelling with his employer, Mozart decided to become a freelance musician in Vienna in 1781, greatly to his father's annoyance.

A stream of masterpieces flowed from Mozart's pen throughout the 1780s including most of his piano concertos along with his greatest symphonies and operas (including *The Marriage of Figaro* and *Don Giovanni*). It was during this period that Haydn told Mozart's father, 'Before God and as an honest man, your son is the greatest composer known to me'.

Mozart's death in 1791 may have been the result of exhaustion. In that one year, he had composed two operas *The Magic Flute* and *La Clemenza di Tito*, two concertos, two quintets and the Requiem.

Carl Maria von Weber (1786–1826) came from a theatrical family (his father was a cousin of Mozart's wife) and Weber, despite his erratic early training, became a keyboard virtuoso at an early age. His first masterpieces were sparkling piano works, full of melodic freshness and romantic energy.

In 1817 Weber took up directorship of the opera house in Dresden and composed his opera *Der Freischütz*. At its first performance in 1821, the new German romantic style with its folk-like melodies and magnificent orchestration (sometimes used to evoke sinister effects) resulted in overnight fame for Weber who began to rival Beethoven as Germany's most celebrated composer.

Weber was already sick with tuberculosis when his final opera *Oberon* was performed in London in 1826. The work received a rapturous response but Weber died the night before he was due to sail home.

Sonatina in A minor

Composed by Georg Benda

D.C. al Fine

9

Für Elise

Composed by Ludwig Van Beethoven

Adagio
(from Piano Concerto No.5 'Emperor')

Composed by Ludwig Van Beethoven

Rondo in A major

Composed by Ludwig Van Beethoven

Allegretto

Sonata in G major, Op.79
(2nd Movement)

Composed by Ludwig Van Beethoven

Bagatelle in G minor, Op.119

Composed by Ludwig Van Beethoven

Allegretto

Sonata in C# minor, Op.27 No.2

('Moonlight Sonata', 1st movement)

Composed by Ludwig Van Beethoven

Adagio sostenuto

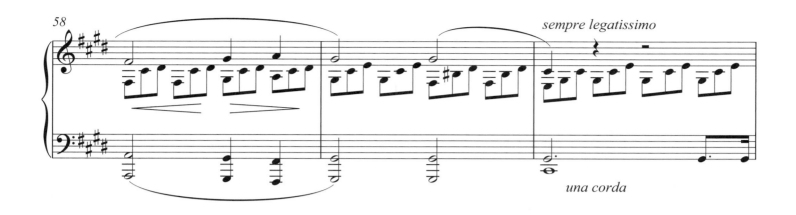

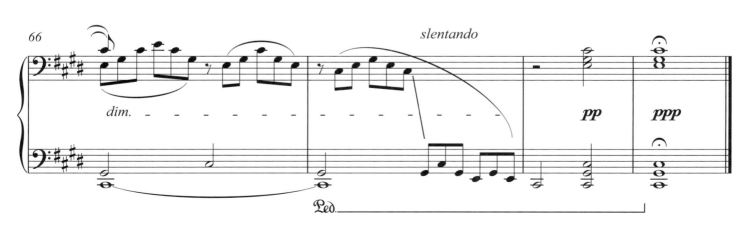

Sonata in C minor, Op.13

('Sonata Pathétique', 2nd movement)

Composed by Ludwig Van Beethoven

rit.   a tempo

Sonatina Op.36 No.1

Composed by Muzio Clementi

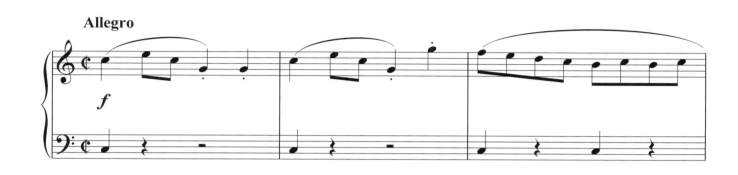

Sonatina Op.36 No.4

Composed by Muzio Clementi

Andante can espressione

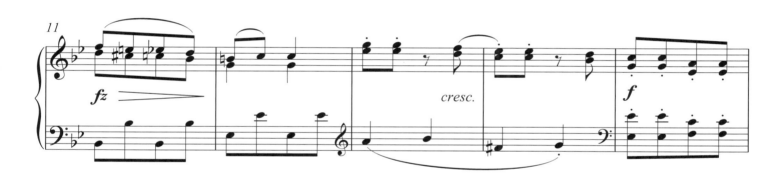

Rondo
Allegro vivace

Fine

D.C. al Fine

Sonatina in G, Op.20 No.1

Composed by Jan Ladislav Dussek

Rondo

Allegretto tempo di minuetto

Maggiore

Dance Of The Blessed Spirits

(from 'Orfeo')

Composed by Christoph Willibald von Gluck

J'ai Perdu Mon Eurydice
(from 'Orfeo')

Composed by Christoph Willibald von Gluck
Arranged by Andrew Skirrow

Sonata in D
(Finale)

Composed by Franz Joseph Haydn

Symphony No.101 'The Clock'
(2nd movement: Andante)

Composed by Franz Joseph Haydn
Arranged by Andrew Skirrow

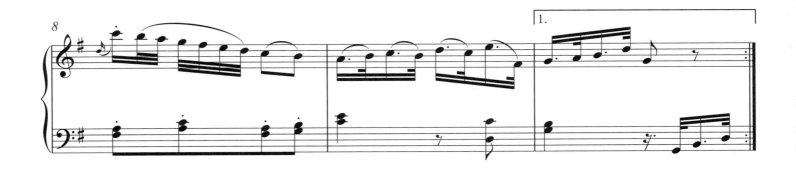

Menuetto Con Variazioni
(from Sonata in D)

Composed by Franz Joseph Haydn

Tempo di Menuetto

Serenade

(from String Quartet Op.3 No.5)

Composed by Franz Joseph Haydn

Arranged by Andrew Skirrow

Andante cantabile

Symphony No.94 'Surprise'

(2nd movement: Andante)

Composed by Franz Joseph Haydn

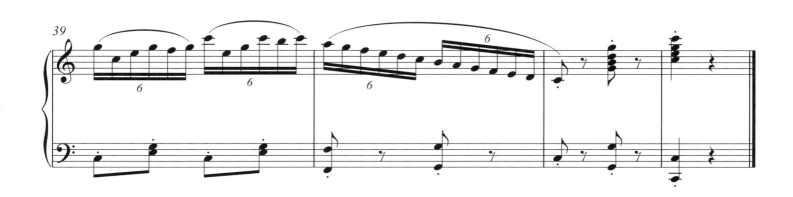

Romance in G, Op.52 No.4

Composed by Johann Nepomuk Hummel

Andante

Playful Dialogue

Composed by Johann Nepomuk Hummel

Moderato

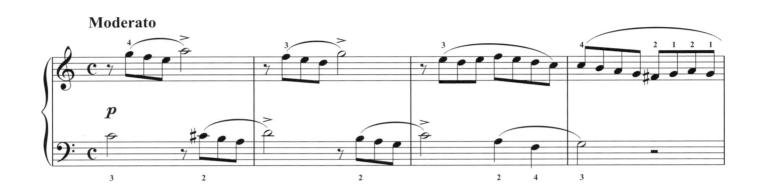

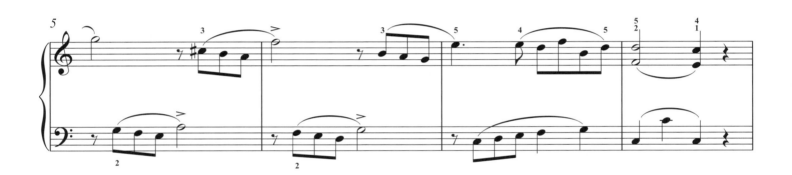

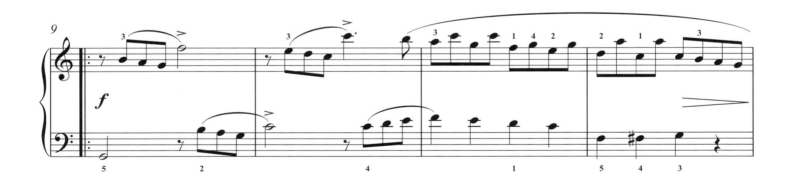

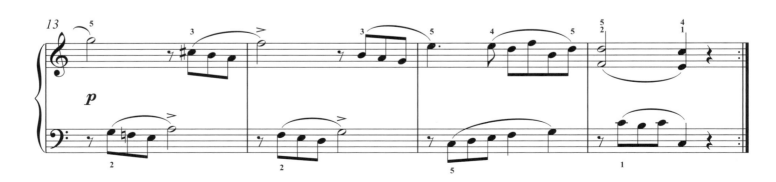

Concerto For Clarinet

(2nd movement: Adagio)

Composed by Wolfgang Amadeus Mozart

Eine Kleine Nachtmusik, K525

(1st Movement)

Composed by Wolfgang Amadeus Mozart

94

Fantasia in D minor

Composed by Wolfgang Amadeus Mozart

Allegretto

Lacrimosa
(from Requiem in D minor)

Composed by Wolfgang Amadeus Mozart

Sonata in C major, K545

Composed by Wolfgang Amadeus Mozart

Andante

Rondo (Allegro)

Piano Concerto No.21 in C major

Composed by Wolfgang Amadeus Mozart

114

Sonata in F major, K280

(1st movement)

Composed by Wolfgang Amadeus Mozart

Variations on "Ah, vous dirai-je Maman"

Composed by Wolfgang Amadeus Mozart

VAR. IV

VAR. V

VAR. VIII
Minore

VAR. IX
Maggiore

131

Voi, Che Sapete
(from 'The Marriage of Figaro')

Composed by Wolfgang Amadeus Mozart

Arranged by Jack Long

Andante con moto

poco cresc.

Sonatina Op.20 No.2

Composed by Friedrich Kuhlau

Adagio e sostenuto

Allegro scherzando

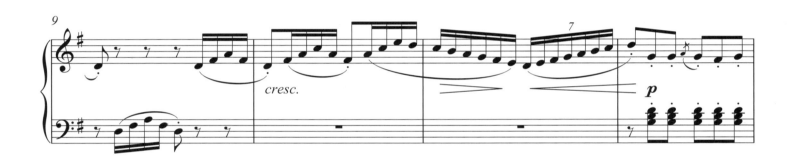

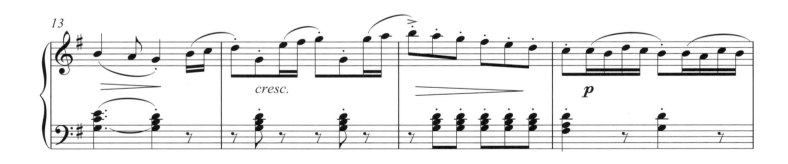

Andante Con Variazione

Composed by Carl Maria von Weber

Variation 2

Variation 3

Sonatine, Op.3 No.1

Composed by Carl Maria von Weber

Moderato e con amore